Sotto Voce

Sotto Voce

Maureen Hynes

Brick Books

Library and Archives Canada Cataloguing in Publication

Title: Sotto voce / Maureen Hynes
Names: Hynes, Maureen, author.
Description: Poems.
Identifiers: Canadiana (print) 20190111690 | Canadiana (ebook) 20190111704 | ISBN 9781771315128 (softcover) | ISBN 9781771315142 (PDF) | ISBN 9781771315135 (ePUB)
Classification: LCC PS8565.Y63 S68 2019 | DDC C811/.54—dc23

We acknowledge the Canada Council for the Arts, the Government of Canada through the Canada Book Fund, and the Ontario Arts Council for their support of our publishing program.

Canada Council   Conseil des arts   **Canadä**   ONTARIO ARTS COUNCIL
for the Arts   du Canada   CONSEIL DES ARTS DE L'ONTARIO

The author photo was taken by Joan Guenther.
The book is set in Dante.
The cover image is "Simple Forms #3" by Bob Hainstock, used by his kind permission.
Design and layout by Marijke Friesen.
Printed and bound by Coach House Printing.

Brick Books
115 Haliburton Road
London, Ontario N6K 2Z2

www.brickbooks.ca

For Ruth Kazdan

Sotto voce Literally, Italian for "under the voice"; in English "under the breath," "in an undertone," "in a private manner." In opera or theatre, the phrase instructs a cast member to step out of the action to address the audience about what's taking place onstage. Instead of raising the voice, the performer intentionally lowers it to emphasize the truth.

CONTENTS

speaking for sky

motherspeak

what she hears

*Song of
Disquiet*

Into the Humber River

Someone tore the hands off a big round clock, familiar
as a classroom compass & abandoned it
to the weeds. It took the time right out of us, poured
it through the small black circle in the clock's
centre & underground into the river.
It was a blessing to watch the hours & minutes
drain away. We didn't miss it the way we'd miss
our own hands. That sudden calm when time
disappears, the atmosphere soupy with fish & bug
& bird busy-ness, the glare of springtime green.
If you spoke into that empty hole, it would hold
your words & breathe them back to you
in the sensible prose of granite & bridge,
in bird vowels, cloud song, river.

Inside My Quietness

after Frank O'Hara and Margaret Christakos

Inside my quietness is a breath
caught in fear. Inside my breath is a warmth
licking the hard forsythia buds yellow. Within
the four-spiked blossoms are a long sleep
and an abundant hunger and inside any hunger
is a woman or rather any woman contains
many hungers. Inside all our fears is a reality
both twisted and true. Art lives beside fear—
fear of falling short or overstating, fear
of offending. But courage beckons others
to attend. I haven't mentioned
the sorrow inside quietness, which tries to shrink
but stays huge. Even larger is the sleeping.
The sleeping body that breathes the world alive.

The Horses, the Sorrow, the Umbilicus

Horses were turned loose in the child's sorrow.
They galloped bare-boned, tore up her imagination's
pasture. Simple things became surreal, malevolent—
a shoelace, a wind-up toy, the cross of a *t*,
or the lost dot in her mother's eye. Grief, continents
to traverse. She hadn't yet seen the tidily grassed graves
at Arras or families rounded up in town squares, poisoned
blankets covering bodies in Haida Gwaii. Sometimes
under the night sky she mounted a mare and rode
into morning, through sunflowered bonfires, through
eulogies and sermons, past incense and tear gas
till she reached the saltwatertide. She never knew if
she had swallowed the sadness through her umbilicus,
joined still to her mother's placental algebra.
The girl sat awhile, gazing out over the waves
to the rising sun, then rapidly dismounted,
looking to her left, looking to her right—

speak now

speak now into the metal mesh
jiggle the puzzle till the parts fall

to the floor   drag the presidents
out for a share of the pain   roll

the dice and scoop the children
out of their sandy shoreline

graves   every era sails
the coffin ships   how many can

the fibreglass boats hold before they
crack in two   mercy is failing

the GPS is failing   speak now

Zodiac

The year and hour break and the day and hour also break so
the year and month have a punishing conflict. World politics
and economies will have setbacks, arguments and controversies.
—"Year of the Fire Rooster," *The Toronto Star*,
January 28, 2017

You enter the hour with diligence and pour
the finest white sand into its glass, then shatter it
with inattention. Once the hour is splintered
into shards on the floor, what can it hold?
And what does it mean to break the year—
more easily busted than an hour, or rather,
its destruction clearer from a great distance.
The same is true of beauty: *The visibility is stunning,*
said the pilot flying us over Grand Canyon.
You can smash a decade with a tsunami,
a genocide, or civil war. An Aleppo can travel
forward in time, bombs falling for generations.

What I Meant

When I said dust, I was thinking of the path
up the steep Andean foothill beyond the Chilean
vineyard. Not housework. When I said

clay, I was thinking of scooping it up in mussel shells
from Lake Simcoe where I tried to make small figures
without baking them into hardness. No wheel or kiln or caliper.

When I said star, I didn't mean gold or brass, but those fellow
night-sky travellers who have seen so much
more than us. When I said hut, I didn't mean

beehive or shed or lean-to, though I could have.
When I said God, I meant dream or myth or sanctifying
presence. Or oppression.

April 1 lune

daybreak a naked
window for
a cold flannel sky

walk out into threat
downed wires spark
intersection throbs

subway woman in
a beige suit
a headwound at the hairline

could be anything

asking the doctor
why my eyes water
redden   ache

why I see police
everywhere
underneath it all

can't get the poet's
book about another
murdered woman

out of my head

How Spring Begins

Is it for miracles
We live?
—James Schuyler

Tags of songs, like salvaged buttons,
always coming undone in my mind, buttonhole
stitches unravelling. Titles jotted down,
melodies saved to mark recurrent
momentary happiness and deepening
sadness, the day the secret fifth season starts,
and the extra month that is sometimes
granted to the faithful and the few.

The beginning of each new season
imparts a gift, like the shirtless child
we saw on Christie Street today, a soccer
ball under his pale arm. Or the frozen
wallet we pried from a hillside in a park
on Monday. Mouldy stench poured out,
the mark of a thief who kept the money
and cashable plastic but tossed into the bushes
the useless hospital cards and religious medal
within. *Mary of the Miracles!* wept
the older woman when my friend returned
her wallet with the medal that kept her
Slovenian father safe
through World War One.

What colours stained that semi-frozen
hillside—mud-muck and filth-stricken ice,
bare-stalk straw. I hate miracles,
the lottery of them, the triumphant song,
their refusal to become humdrum,
predictable, the way they overlook
the deserving, the praying poor,
the terminally ill. Even though
there's no denying them, I poured out
my family's bottle of Lourdes water
all around our Manitoba maple.

Song of Disquiet

How high in the air to hold the baton? What note
to begin with? On the downstroke, the key
of sorrow or sigh? Reader, do you hear
a low-pitched wing-flap, the bird of paradise
landing on the rainforest zipline whose seams
are stitched to hell? Let's listen for
the quiver, the tone of leaf-tremble
that monarch multitudes set off as they gather
in the oyamel firs of Michoacán, the note
hovering in the heat just beyond
the lava-covered church buried to midway
up its steeple.

When you settle, what chord
accompanies you, and is it monotonous or tragic?
Reader, the light dims early here and a single day
brings hail, brings ice underfoot—
too little snow to lie on, angels impossible, too little
hail to hold in your cold fingers and just enough rain
to soften the abandoned wasps' nest hanging
from bare branches. Is this a winter song?

I laughed aloud

in the middle of the night
and told you, *Too complicated to explain.*
A few of us gathered, writing
letters to our ancestors who
can no longer hear but still can read
messages if written in thin chocolate ink
on a surface of rosewater-scented cake or bread
split open on a tabletop to be photographed
or scanned, transmitted back
in time. My question to them

a redundancy, but nightly the stars
repeat themselves, fade, and return—
Do you like to use words, or something
obvious or foolish like that.

You and I, we sleep in the prescribed
north-south direction, our bodies
aligned to each other and to the stylus
Sappho holds against her lips—
thoughtful, open-eyed. With her we look
up at the mountain of dreamquestions
and down into the sleepvalley.

Ancestors

The dog next door distant as her masters.
From their garden, she looks up at me
in my window and looks away. No

bond between us.
But her dark gaze sinks into me
nonetheless. In exile, Bei Dao writes,

each and every moment's a shortcut—
of course, that's a translation from
the Chinese, but what is that moment

of looking away a shortcut into?
Bei Dao may have meant a quick detour
to death, but I should probably consider

moments like the black dog's single
bark at the approach of her teenaged
mistress. A deep bark of *yes*.

My arms stretch from my second floor
balcony down to my neighbour's
back door, my fingers scratch behind

the dog's ears. Her name recalls a distant
island. Is she far from her wolf ancestors?
Perhaps she knows mine are panthers.

Twenty Naked Selves

after Frank O'Hara

I am an ill-clad Venetian artist who has fallen
in love with the winter streets of Montreal
and the snow-laden branches in its parks.
I am a buried electric bulb awaiting
the full moon after the first day of spring,
which is today. I am a kitchen fanatic,
a short-order cook, not a pastry chef. Or perhaps
I am a pastry chef—look at my *croquembouche*—
not a cook. This is like the discussion that
you must love either science fiction or mysteries,
not both and definitely not neither. Of course
I love neither. I am one of the Irish volunteers
now boxed into a Dublin graveyard. I am
an enthusiastic and hesitant teacher.
A linguist, walking the paths of Père Lachaise,
speaking, as the songbirds do, a different
language with each season and exiting the graveyard
to find a father easing his child's foot into a sneaker
and taking him on a rough sea crossing.
I am a delighted aunt, a delighted passenger,
a delighted lover. These are not permanent states.
I am a seamstress stitching plackets and hems
into poems, escape hatches. I am a cyclist
spinning across the city after my machine's
tune-up at the spring rate offered
if you book before this leap year's extra day,

which I did. I squeezed a lot into it.
I am a colourist in a hair salon, a potter, a heretic.
A non-driver and an air traffic controller
monitoring the earthbound messages of stars
and satellites. An asthmatic like Proust, but
less prolific. Listening to your footfalls, I am
a sentimental philatelist, collecting the stamps
you make on the stairs, the kitchen floor,
the ravine path, the leaf- and twig-
covered soil of our backyard.

Sotto Voce

after David Lang's the whisper opera

When you whisper everything, when even

your saxophone whispers its notes, when you just
graze your fingertips across the drumskin for a drumly

quietness, or the words on your sheet lower their volume

to minimal, when you forswear *aloud*
for the everyday language of small rivers (today

the Don is open, free-flowing and black, not closed

and frozen white), when the scratchy hushes under
the thickening ice become fainter and fainter,

when you whisper everything, vows and regrets,

sweet nothings and morsels of shame, or just the abundant
mundanities of your life—listeners strain to catch

your watery drift, they follow your eyes. Your breath

is a hand resting on a baby's naked chest.
After the breath stops, Spicer says, *the words listen.*

At the end of the evening's whispering,

an old neighbour said all she could hear was the eulogy
for her mother from thirty years ago.

You are always hearing your own

all the way down past the future,
louder and more audible than murmurs that *go swimming*

past you as if they were blue fish.

Breathing Lessons

With a fingernail

                     or a crochet hook
or an iris stem you can write messages
on my skin—word-welts that flower
for an hour, then fade. Draw spirals or
outline a map of the Great Lakes.
Dermatographia, that condition of skin
awfully sensitive to scratches and scrapes—
what priests and doctors called *witch skin,*
sign of a woman possessed or
insane.

          If on my inner arm you spell out
the names of the months you are spending
in hospital after your heart surgery, or
write the long Latin names
of your two infections—*Staphylococcus aureus*
and *Klebsiella pneumoniae,* the high
degrees of your daily fevers,
and the exact number of worried nights,
none will be permanent.
They will fade after a brief eruption,
a spell, a squall, a cloud, a leaf, a laugh.

Pebble

                The pebble she takes
into her mouth is a pill for the pain settling in.
Dime-sized, a single white line across its grey
flatness on her tongue, it clicks against her teeth.
The headache is returning like her mother's
interminable phone calls.
                Speak to the mother,
she tells herself. Smooth her hair, massage her scalp.
Scratch her back, oil her heels and soles. Talk her back
to her young motherhood when she bought
a French serge suit—pencil skirt, fitted flared jacket.
Slash pockets, their seams stitched closed. A mother who
never took scissors to the threads, never allowed herself
the pleasure of putting her hands in her pockets.
That would *ruin the line*.
                Damselfly, she thinks,
come stitch my mind shut so the headache won't return.
Daisy, glimmer the ache away. Black-winged cormorant,
she calls, soar over the river's suspension bridge
and past the creosote-scented railway ties,
bring me your recipe for calm
in a clamshell, in narrowing swoops
bind a birch-white bandage around my head.

concoction

finger the bumps & whorls of the ginger root
steep it into your tea   savour its slender slices
burning your throat   blend sage with melted
beeswax & smooth onto your bare breasts
grind amethyst geodes into dust   swirl
into cinnamon oil   rub into your scalp
make a gelatin of ground eucalyptus bark
& spray gathered at the foot of Niagara Falls
cut frayed silk into ribbons   knit them
into mittens   catch a baby's first murmurs
on your old cassette recorder   let them loose
on a subway car   rest your hand on a rusty railing
until the crusted oxides etch a pointillism
onto your palm

breathing lessons

she read the word *wishlessness* to us
match it   she said   to your pace & gait
don't arrow your intentions into the world
just wander from flower to flower   fish to fish

we pulled ourselves back into infancy
took to opening wide our eyes
gasping   yawning   sighing   blowing   howling
what would you relearn if you could

knit together the fontanelles of what's remembered   stroll
flaneur-like along avenues of lost languages
sway like a fearsome dancer or leap like a dancing fear
shiver   then crumble like a leaf
those too are breathing lessons

⋆

the cocrico   squawky national bird   landed on Tobago's
currency & disappeared as quickly as any currency does
inspiration is really just a matter of
breath   I said & put aside my puffer

is there enough longing in the poem too much caution
beauty & desire surrounded us like a turquoise sea
on either side of the peninsula   lapping at my feet was the remorse
felt by fathers & daughters   their failed gaze & recollection

would you restore both if you could
        I think I would
she wrapped her hands around my wrists
        she lowered me gently to the ground
regret cushioned me

In Solitary

after the exhibition Mary Pratt *at the McMichael Art Gallery, 2014*

My only strength is finding something
where most people would find nothing.
—Mary Pratt

Today, my love, you took me to see
her work, her strictest realism—
glassy apples in a bowl, a new microwave
raised high and lit like an altar. Remember
her half-dozen eggshells atilt
and cracked, albumen
strings glinting? Perhaps,

as she said, she misnamed *Eggs in an Egg Crate*
because she had just lost twins. Her glowing
jars of jelly: the startlingly arduous task—
hot and somewhat dangerous, careful spill of boiling
coral. I know I've written of crabapples before

but their dauntlessness and durability
remind me of our love: staying red even when
unpicked all winter. Those wizened ampersands
hanging from snow-threaded branches, black
umlaut seeds within. A lifetime's hard work,
she said, underlining her loneliness—

and also today, my love, Hurricane died. Did he feel
freed from cancer's prison? Left a deathbed wish
for yet one more of the wrongfully convicted,
all *innocent as witches*. In solitary for years—
so many sacrifices he didn't choose, yet
the *something* he found where so many of us
would find nothing.

Keep It Dark

Who are the goddesses who fell in love
with each other? Which ones were celebrated
or punished with stardom—captives
hoisted into the sky to cast nets of light
from the inner surface of our night-dome?
Go ask Alice B, ask Ms. Stein, ask Djuna,
Frances and Florence. Or just listen

to those goddesses on Duncan's windowsill
boasting about their skill with poisons,
flaunting fierce lineages, family troubles
as vengeful as Lear's. Here's the nymph
Callisto, who welcomed Diana's embraces
without knowing it was really Zeus
taking the huntress's form to

enter her, break her vow. How to punish
her for the pregnancy? Turn her into
a bear—so we call her Ursa Major.
But is it forcing things to say
she preferred Diana to Zeus? We're always
looking backwards in galleries and books
to find women like ourselves. *Keep it dark,*

wrote the anonymous photographer
to the four smiling women in suits and ties
in the photo she called *The Queer Quartette.*
Decades ago, two couples at dinner in a resort—

the Laurentians, say, or the Adirondacks.
Even on a moonless night, Callisto
still knows their names.

A State of Undress

for the ten women of the Beaver Hall Group

Glaring colours and rough drawing,
said the male critics. *Big ideas*
and almost no means, your followers said.
Brothers and fiancés off to the Great War,
you turned away from grief, painted
blocks of colour, portraits
of other women: a bather with fleshy
open legs, a girl in a dotted dress,
two young theatre-goers with their backs
to us. And the nude with sandals on—
Not a proper nude, said the judge
removing the work from display,
merely a state of undress.

Your lives the subject of your work, work
your lives' mainstay, friendships
the engine. I've known so many
groups like yours—for me, it's been late-night
calls across the continent,
cooking up conferences for four hundred,
wrangling meetings and readings
and petitions. Or just four women laughing
over breakfast in a restaurant by a pond,
notebooks at the ready.

For you, storefronts and snow-clad
city streets your daily vistas.
Eliminating distractions, simplifying
life, but painting sex, flesh into bold clarity.
Well turned out, you indulged in high fashion,
a simple coif, plain gold chain at the neck.
And O, how a model described the woman
who painted her portrait: *Like a dreamy*

purring kitten, velvety and luxurious—
pretty sure I know what that means.

Inside Hazel

Hurricane Hazel, 1954

The morning after that hurricane, eighty-one dead.
My father drove us to the ravine's edge where
the small city-tamed river below had surged,
swallowed buildings, collapsed bridges.
Half a house crumpled into the river, an outer
wall sheared off, cross-sectioned
like my dollhouse, but enormous and aloft.
No one died here, but did that family
ever sleep again? We looked up
to the second floor, floral wallpaper around
a bathroom sink and mirror, two red
towels hanging on a towel rack.

Usually, when a tsunami or a forest fire turns
inside out, what tumbles free are widows and crushed
limbs, a wooden trestle bridge burned to blackest ash,
an ocean fear-stained by nuclear waste.
But inside Hazel was also born a lifelong
romance—a hurricane that stopped the train
in its tracks for hours and that's where
Jane and Helen, two teachers at the same
academy, found they were more
than colleagues, began a forty-five-year journey.

Staying Away from the Grand River

The river was sour then, not yet sugared
by saccharine and sucralose or her declarations.
We were searching for a double bed
over the bubbling gorge in a town
full of strangers who *knew*. A few years ago,
you might have been beaten up, said a friend.
Something witch-like in us though we stayed
far from the river. Icy paths cordoned off
and the sound of crashing water beyond
the evergreens. All those winter visits
to scenic towns with someone blinded
and blinding. Another love, part of
a suite of unsuitables. I have a photo
of the first, but many more of my sweeter,
much more sustaining love.

its many uses

could you spin fear on a lathe
shape it into something useful & pretty
place a candle inside & light it

is fear a stone or liquid or just an oily
mishmash   a vapour that fevers through
skin & gut & frontal lobe

could you spread it like broadloom
on your floors   use its electrons to warm
your feet   sharpen your intellect

how opaque it becomes   how it fans out
visible to all   shivering iridescence
like a peacock's tail

could you run yards of it through your sewing
machine   stitch shimmery curtains
for every member of your family

while you're at it   make handbags & light bulbs
scooters & socks & minute doses of medicine
to calm the jittery heart

how old is fear   could you find its original form
display it in a gilt frame & sell it for millions
in an auction house

shape it into bricks & fire them in a kiln
bombproof them   lay new foundations
in Basra for bridges & homes & hospitals

could you melt fear in a double boiler   use it
to frost a cake you serve on a banana leaf   one
banquet ingredient among many   but if you

rolled it into tiny seeds no birds would touch it

Fearless

We are staining our fingers with turmeric,
burning our throats with sambal.
We are swallowing aspirins and blueberries.
When we travel, we always choose
the window seat, the better to feel the tilt
of a landing over a rocky shoreline.
Who knows, we think, our lost eyeglasses,
rings, lovers may be just around the next sharp
corner. We have seen wars change form
and persist despite the songs from old musical
scores. We are reading gilt-edged pages from
books in Cyrillic and stitching them into
mukluks and parkas, pasting them onto Turkish
blue walls. Some of us have gotten good news
from peeing on a stick. There has been dancing.
We are writing of infection and illness
and artists of every genre. How a head
of lettuce fed a hungry audience for many nights,
how a mother's illness ravages her brain
but does not soften her heart.
The shadow of a cross falls into an intersection.
How the Star Hotel swallowed a father
and a phantom ship carried a grandmother
to Morocco, a white convertible awaited
a brother. A hurricane upended
another city. Haunted by the childhood
sight of a home for unwed mothers, by a window view
of city trees, by a sister's faded nightie.

We are sustained by white foods—pierogies,
cod, cauliflower, milk. We are washing
our bodies and souls at the mouth
of an industrial river. We are getting intimate
and alphabetical. An aurora of metaphor
is glowing in our minds and its source
is the cardamom-scented river of our tears.

ajoupa 2

the airline passage parched & scoured her—
       she'd rather have sailed home on a liner
small dry leaves travelled back with her
       stashed in half-filled notebooks & memoirs
of daughters whose mothers had suicided   of the son whose father's
       bones were disappeared into powder   but the wooden
poles of the ajoupa recalled Agrigento   its marble pillars standing
       above those fallen to the ground
in her luggage she stored enlivening oils
       rustle & scent   of hibiscus   jasmine   chaconia
after-images of yellow-&-black sugar birds   flitting
       onto her breakfast table   pinching beakful after beakful of sugar
the breakers summoning & releasing her breath
       calming her nights   her morning visits to the sea
simply lifting her arms   into the rainless sky

speaking
for sky

speaking for sky

I don't want to play favourites
with the elements   but earth
is my task this autumn

sumac   rickrack   parched fields

though mostly I want to speak
for sky   its embrace of open land
green tablet   legible surface

we could go large or small with sky

flex & flatten the small of the back   starfish stretch
arms & legs   increase presence of self
between sky & earth   when upright our bodies

ignore sky   lying down
body speaks to sky   sky replies in kind
milk-white draw of cloud pouring & pouring

the sentence   a contrail   written across the sky

sky filled with metal & fumes & noise heard
before the aircraft appears   except for the dirigible
& its inflated beer ads   hanging above city traffic

so loud in its silence

within & beneath sky   the kinds of madness
that displacement brings   prime farmland
left fallow   a refugee child asleep in a Hungarian ditch

the dispersals   these lands have seen

where once human bones   were laid
Wendat & settlers
their feasts   their crops   their homes

daylight   nightfall   starspill
untidy hopes rain-washed   snow-covered
resilience & daring   coltsfoot   may apples

calamus root to protect the heart

the land is a tablet   never empty of words
a table   a place   a plate at a table   a plat
for orchards   bee balm   redwings

what the farmer writes   & rewrites

Derailment Ode Several Cars Long

for the people of the expropriated Pickering lands

1

If I could re-lay the torn-out tracks and cross ties
from my city to your lands, if I could run new trains
between us, restock those cargo spaces with edibles,
drinkables, every kind of unfrightening freight;
if I could guard the rail yards, the grades and inclines,
reframe the farmlands with trails, barn dances,
and winning glances, I would be thirty minutes from you,
we could ride back and forth between your home and mine.

2

This entire land has been tied with tracks, then untied
and untracked. Lines laid at great human cost across
looted lands, then torn out one by one—another kind of
derailment, not just this summer's at the foot of my street
that brought a new diesel and creosote stink,
but also the cries of sumac trees chainsawed away,
serviceberry shrubs pulled out, blackberry and elderberry
that edged the tracks and fed the red-winged blackbirds.
Now the mockingbird, whose first visit this April
covered every other songbird's song, has fled his perch
on the high hydro tower beside the railbeds.

3

How can humans be such creative destroyers, such
destructive creators? Seated in the circle around
matzoh and wild rice, apple slices and almonds—
in the Abundance ceremony this autumn,
I hoped for reversals. For clarity,
foresight, inner vision, outer presence.
I asked for too much from that one afternoon—
justice and plenty, an end to discord and hardship
on these rich, twice-stolen lands.

Sonnenizio on the Unseen

Even before I saw the chambered nautilus,
and that was only in the vast and blinking online sea—
or perhaps I did see it in one of Neruda's houses
because all his homes draw marvel-seekers—
even before that, I heard the armoured cicada sawing
during a Chinese summer exactly how they saw back home
and felt the gaze of a serious young seaman
inking a scrimshaw boat into a Pleistocene tusk.
Before not-seeing gilt altars and guilted children
or the massacre of west coast walruses and seals,
I said the unseen is what will undo us, not so much
what is out of sight but what we refuse to see—
it will seed the future into our bodies, raise walls and beams,
and seal us from each other with hardened pearly seams.

Preventorium

High Park is home to sleepers. Voles and night herons
and readers adrift over sentences in books,
fox sparrows and drowsy bison in the zoo.
Homeless women, their swollen legs outstretched.
Seeds and roots and corms, babies in their strollers,
snakes in their hibernacula under the city's quilted snow.

The park's nature centre is the old open-air Forest School—
on its wall, the most calming photo of sepia slumber:
daytime rows of girls sleeping in cots, curtains of shade
pulled around them. How I want to join them,
fall back nine decades into one of those cots;
how I envy their striped blankets and piped blazers,

their teacher with her hair pulled up onto her head,
a loose bird's nest and a tight knot at the centre
like a searched-for egg. We call this shallow time,
its surface nearly the thickness of a moth's wings.
In those days, we shunned hybridity. We divided and subdivided—
inside and outside, poor and rich, sick and healthy,

hungry and well-fed, dirty and clean (all those sinks),
safety and danger. We still do, but the school was supposed
to pull children from one to the other, prevent TB,
repair their *wasted little bodies*. In good weather,
between lessons and sports and chores, a daily two-hour outdoor
nap. In their sleep, the girls make perfect clay pots, sketch

lynxes and leopards, sail across glinting waters,
plough the skies in a biplane. One girl is dreaming
she has got her breath back to play the penny
whistle with her grandfather. Beneath them all,
the river's deep time slowly flows and flows. Then
chocolate milk and the trip back home on a streetcar.

Our Own Myths

We make our own myths and spells
these days—clear-cut myths of peeled bark
and planed logs, rooted myths for abandoned lands,
their owners evicted and bereft. Tell backhoe fables
to conjure dwellings whole and complete
back onto these fields and flatlands. Undo spells
cast by profiteers, sing new songs
of undoing and renewing,
miracles of restoration accomplished
by the heroic and the flawed.

Today we joined the rebel women
who still walk rebel lands, women who
never said no to the crow, their ears attuned
to salmon spawning in Duffins Creek,
apples ripening in orchards, sap reddening
the willow branches every spring. Old and young
women, each with one hand on a steering wheel,
the other on a keyboard. Or one hand pulling
a cabbage from the kitchen garden, the other
playing a harmonica for the disappeared
children, grown and gone, tossed
from their parents' lands.

Little Rouge Creek

rusted-railing bridge
sloping up in its centre
where you stand
first facing upstream   then
downstream
                you take the river's

ripples   pliés   knots
into your arms   legs   spine
& skull   return them in
an awkward dance
but still   the sun pours
the last moments of summer

over the ridge
dogs & an accordion   (why not?)
& the family   who comes yearly
pours *vin rouge*   onto the ground
honours the uncle   whose ashes
lie in the Galapagos & the Antarctic
who went wayfaring
for Greenpeace

out of sight   the road named
for the township's wealthiest settler
not for those he dispossessed
their languages almost forgotten

in the search   for lost names
hope confronts despair

you join a human flock
sixty people dance   a wingless landing
into the farmer's yard
huge maples surround the clearing

Prescribed Burn

At the entrance to High Park, a yellow flyer
stapled to the post proclaims
a planned oratorio to be conducted

by the High Complexity Burn Boss.
Qualified instrumentalists will fan out
with drip torches, dropping flame

on leaf litter. The crabgrass will not
be harmed, nor the ground-nesting
cellophane bees. The contained burn

will singe the shrubs and brush, its song
will preserve the black oak savannah,
but the Burn Boss warns smoky arias

will rise above the surrounding
neighbourhood. If they don't disperse,
says the flyer, close your windows against

the dissonant cloud, leave. The wood ducks
and great horned owl have been warned
separately.
                    We search for the Burn Boss

to request a crescendo to clear each corner
of our lives. Char the leaf litter, restore the open
tall grass area to euphony and hope.

693 Cemetery Road

We lived a week in the slope-ceilinged, head-hitting house,
banged our knees against the banister, nailed pillows
to the rafters, abandoned our books in the sand.
Spilled every kind of tea, crushed blueberries to mask
our bruises. Sunrise pierced our eyes awake. The sky

filled and emptied, fog surrounded the bed, curtained
our lovemaking. Once a day we briefly tuned into drought
across the land, strife on the convention floor.
We cooked outdoors—scallops, turnips, rhubarb pie—
and folded ten-dollar bills into herons and pelicans.

We found companions. A shabby-winged eagle perched
on a post, presided over our seaside holiday. Quick
visits from a hare family. One evening, a stillness with ears
stopped and moved and stopped: through dusk's thick fog,
nine deer in the tall grasses, staring at us.

Behind the house, a cemetery. Beyond, the world's
calmest ocean. Villagers had pulled tombstones out
from the dense alder, bayberry, and rugosa, scrubbed
till the old Swiss-German names appeared. Rearranged
the stones in a harmonious new order that renamed

those lying below, children and women who died young,
men who lived long. Tidying the dead. We walked miles

of beaches daily, burned the bashed tops of our heads. Tides puddled at our ankles, soaked our thoughts. The dead lent us their sleep each night. And when we woke, we thanked them.

motherspeak

motherspeak

. . . Take not
away from me the small fires
I burn in the memory of love.
—John Wieners

it's the day for mothers   to speak
gratitude or bitterness or relief
into the static of old telephone lines

it is not a day   for small fires   votive lamps
yahrzeit candles   the cinder of my mother's
cigarette   a fiery beast is devouring

a boreal forest   the northern half of a province
it's a day   for the motherless & under-mothered
to speak our orphan words   to lift the lily of the valley's

tiny teacups to our lips   to wash the chandelier's
crystal droplets   how rough the towels
how stiff the sheets   the mothers have left us

this morning the wind whistled   into the speaker's
megaphone   she listed her several workplace injuries
her children's names   showed us an image

of a Hindu holy woman   & a picture of the judge
who denied her claims   we tossed our words
up seven storeys   to the blankness

of the politicians' Sunday absence   how sallow
was the sky   how gusty the wind
the colossal fires still burning

A Taxonomy of Troubles

                    Still trying to understand
the hunger that makes wasps sting and fathers strike,
how the awl shudders into the soft
cured skin of a goat. What makes the eye
look away and how the injured heart
can muscle into someplace new, somewhere
shining but askew. How silliness and sorrow
can drop from the same cloud
and how exactly the breeze cools. The size
of the world's container for mercy.
                    Why the word *welcome*
is so difficult to utter and whether big-
heartedness can be contagious
in a time of forced labour, barrel bombs,
razor wire, drowning. What a late
pregnancy feels like and what exactly
a baby sees and hears in utero.
Across Budapest, Gabor Maté said,
                    all the Jewish newborns (and he was one)
were wailing the week the Nazis
invaded. Mothers were feeding
distress into their babies' mouths and everyone's
capacity for grace forever jeopardized.
                    Is bearing witness all
I can do when my life has been nearly
untouched? Is witness enough? Tonight
the horizon is a dividing line between
two shades of cobalt. How can I watch
slavery's pyramid be reconstructed.

octopus

at breakfast the woman offered her toddler son
her breast   he swallowed channels of moon milk
& borrowed the cartoon creatures' eight-armed travels

their dexterity & intelligence   beneath
the lunar lens the heart attends more carefully
to our troubles than we've ever dreamt   last week

my friend's heart knew what her brain was sleeping
through   tried to stop beating as her tumourous
breast was removed   tried to keep the pairing

intact   unhalf the halving   the essential
twinning & twining our bodies make
the child coiled four twist-ties together into

another octopus   fell asleep in his mother's arms

newborn

Dreams reveal
how much in danger we are
—John Wieners

the danger   that I would not
recognize her   that I could not

keep her   the nurse carried
my newborn   out of the hospital room

from my bed I called out   *paint*
her baby toe red   so I'll know her

craving certainty   she was truly mine
a shiver of cold paint   covering

my own toe   woke me up
why didn't I say   *bring her back*

Apollo

Think of it as a blanket, said the rabbi at the graveside.
So first we spread the light brown clay-soil
over the man whose eyes had been so bright and heart
so warm. Then the sky dropped a nubbly sheet,
snow falling in huge flakes, pines tall above the polished
casket. Oh, tell me something hopeful—tell me
again about the baby born this week,
the baby whose parents named him Apollo because
they love the sound of the name. At the shiva
we welcomed the baby, the return of the god
of art, remedy, and repair. Kaddish and cream
cheese, photo albums and scotch whisky,
new coats, old boots, everyone in black and white.
A week of thundersnow over the lake and threats
of flooding. The warmth leaked out of our house,
the furnace heart failed, or rather the secondary
heat exchanger cracked and temperatures dropped
day and night. Show me again the photo of the day-old
baby wrapped in his woolly yellow blanket.

The Ballad of a Good Night's Sleep

The snowy owl turning in its flight
shears sleep out of air, lays a nighttime
web of tracks for your mind to cross.
Whitecaps break against your rest,

morning, dusk, or afternoon. The nurse calls,
she's spread jelly on your toast, poured chamomile tea
into your cup. Sleep eludes you—or do you resist
sleep? In the cracked glass of your dreams

you count the notes in each repeating chord,
how many measures in this relief? You painted
watercolours of icebergs melting, flower stalls in Chile,
the palest weed-straws poking out of roadside snows.

Inside your now abandoned shed—
your bookshelves and paints, photos and flowers,
your daybed for respite, for floating back
to memories of whales and Walden Pond.

Toxins and treatments, nurses and restless nights.
Darkened skies open and close with the heartbeats
of the sleepless. We have melted the seven
medications for the ill and innocent

into candle wax, shaped it into a small warm
oval and pressed it against your forehead
over your third eye, to dim the glare
of the night light at the foot of your bed.

Dearest friend,

shouldn't we write down our smallest, most honest
questions, courier them to our friends and family,
require monthly replies so that vast rips and holes
caused by all the questions we didn't ask
won't torment us lying awake after their deaths?
Dearest friend, am I indulging my sorrow?

Your long sickness, your early departure. Troubled
turning seventy in a way you'd never been birthday-troubled before:
always a shout of gladness for another year to dive into.
O if I could have kept you here with crabapple jelly, I would have
pilfered fruit from every tree in the county, stood over boiling pots
of coral-coloured steam through heatwave days and lightning nights.

Dearest friend, we had so many long and urgent conversations—
gripes and gardens and grandchildren; *must-read* lists; how to transform
disappointment into art. Could I not unlock those hours
from some vault or archive, take them out and redeem them
the way you pawned an old diamond ring from your safety

deposit box to get some money for a single mother? Those hours
now treasure cached in some great chieftain's
burial chamber, holding not whetstones and sceptres,
Celtic bowls and tosses of gold coins inside ivory purses,
but your wit and talent for friendship. O the evergreen riches.

Phonograph

The photo turns her hair a strange new
colour—almost henna-rinsed—and casts
her eyes upward, seemingly in prayer

as if star music lures her gaze
towards last night's eclipse
for a brief galactic tour that nearly cured

her of shattered vows and Lenten bribes.
Is she recalling the wind-up phonograph
at the old cottage, where the dock slides

into the tiniest lake imaginable, a half-
scoop of ice-age water that drowned
a canoe, a friend, a loon's night laugh?

Three small splashes, three unrecorded sounds.

Luminosity

By the time we look up we might have lost
enough star power to end a small war on Earth.
Frittering my gaze. All those Mediterranean
gods & goddesses, says my Norwegian friend,
they were so *active*. Banished for their sins
into the galaxy's outer coldness, generating
just enough lumens to teach us a few lessons—
how to endure, how to be present & sparkle,
to hide when we need to, to extend our love
through space, across time.

Ah, those nymphs & monsters, their abductions
& infidelities. Their beam energy.
Remembering that tented night in Zimbabwe
when all I could think was *diamonds,*
black velvet, shuddering at my own
persistent clichés. Then that moment—
a hyena visiting the campground's rim
took a quick dog-look at us & loped off
starwards for other prey. His sparing us
brought me close to our impermanence—
how sudden chance can kill, but not cast us
into the stars. Couldn't we measure
our lives in lumens? I'd be happy to have,
on a scale from one to five, anything brighter
than the second magnitude.

Hourges Orchard Cemetery

we visited your grave   saw the date
        your wooden cross freshly whitened
        your name   hand lettered in black paint   or
was it etched into a headstone
        ohh   this was 39 years ago
        and you'd died 60 years earlier
there were no fruit trees   no spring blossoms
        just a small crop   144 soldiers planted
        I listened for your young man's voice
heroic   wrote the captain in his citation
        I hope he wrote that to your mother too
        not the rest of his report
a little bit of trouble that day   15 dead
        you survived Vimy   but then a year later—

we have become specialists in death-dealing
        Cornelius   so much worse in the 100 years since
        but the family fact of your death overshadows
how you must have done your share
        how can the words of Greek gods & goddesses
        25 centuries old pursue us   but yours are lost
can we not read a few of your letters sent home
        pour a drop of oil into your palm   hum to your bones
        I want to lay a small flowered rug
on your plot   cushion & warm you   set it apart
        give pause to cemetery visitors
        I have never made a song that told of war
wrote H. D.   how can we keep those songs unsung

dolorosa

for some   Holy Week   the week of processions & penitence
ends with forsythia & the blue spill of scilla
all down this winter-battered city hill

for others, bombardment & catastrophe
Stabat Mater at the foot of the cross
Stabat Mater dolorosa

the second-deadliest weapon in the arsenal
pitched right up close to the deadliest
stood the woman with her sorrow

at the foot of the motherbomb
we roast the lamb & forget the past
our right to live a blitz-free life

who gathers the hungry children
boils a single egg for a family of eight
who binds their wounds & lifelong distress

who speaks with a stammer & never
learns to read   whose orange life jacket
is cast on the rocks by storm at midnight

after sorrow comes happiness
wrote Ho Chi Minh
what could be more natural

we are in a remembering frame of mind
but it does no good   there are some
who think of war with no despair

who scrawl red words on every wall
we want a map out of here   we have
only the six-petalled blue flower

*what she
hears*

bolt of fabric

it could be Chinese silk
or rough Irish linen   slub & flecks
of applause   tertiary good wishes woven in

possibly woven on the looms of the gods
& goddesses who remove chaff from our fibre
& let us begin our beginnings

yellow strips torn from my dead uncle's unpaid
parking tickets (what he got away with)
plaited into thick padded matting

or braided with my mother's prayed & unprayed
novena cards (her devotion sincere nonetheless)
made into longings & linings & interlinings

you could gather water-lily & alder roots
soften them with your teeth   weave them into a shawl
eight hours a day you could cut three-metre lengths

at your first job   you could wrap your lifetime in it
or at least wear it for the three simple ceremonies

Not Enough

           Yes, forgetting is my subject,
the core of my fears. When the shofar
sounds its yearly reawakening call
from Venice's Spanish synagogue,
built 1542—how many of us can hear it?

           This is the autumn that
leaky boats disgorge seven thousand people
a day onto Greek shores—O Sappho,
do you welcome them? All you
stars and immortals of antiquity, look at
our wars—we learn new weapons,
practise them overhead in cities,
deafen residents and there is no
dancing. Weeping is not enough.

           And sorrow's handle
is too hot to touch. Struggling to grasp
what the burn surgeon said—scars
a sign of strength. Rice pots and frying pans
are my containers, spoons and salves and stitches
my tools. Comfrey and burdock to heal
skin, strengthen hearts.

What Happened to the Danceable Jazz?

Peculiar to wake up into a January
morning so full of roses—dashed
into a florist's yesterday and splurged
eight whole dollars on an iffy but still
impeccably peach-hued bouquet. My gardener
friend says, *It takes a lot of pesticides
to grow a perfect rose.* Does the rose recall
the woman who inhaled toxic spray
in a Colombian greenhouse, who lost
her job when she got pregnant—and then
miscarried? The person who clipped
its thorns, packed, and shipped it?

Hey, buddy, said the dad to his
four-year-old, both walking ahead
of me on Brunswick Avenue, *Hey,
look at this*—pulling a yellow rose
out of the snow-crusted yew hedge
and presenting it long-stemmed
to his son with an overhead arm-swirl.
Maybe an unwanted gift stashed
last night by a woman who spurned
her lover—or the growers—and took it
out on the rose.

Would you like to live your life
as an orangerie or a flower shop?
All that fragrance and beauty, yes—

but then no dancing and so many discards
wilting at the end of every day.
No guarantees, said the woman
behind the counter. *Put the stems
in hot water.* Stern, like that.

I'd like to dance gin-glimmery
into the blue Evening in Paris
mama bottle of perfume, starlit and eva-
nescent, a day dancer a night dancer
with a fireplace of sunset waves
behind us, a little breeze up and glasses
clinking—so much more *pep* than modern jazz—
that big band gardenia sound that lasted
way too long but still faded much too soon.
Tuesday will turn to bitter cold.

February 15

Dear Jack,

When you were writing, no one had yet invented the wind chill factor & it would have made little difference to you anyway, living in San Francisco, where my friend Julie is now visiting & writing me about the magical weather. But today as I walked to the subway in minus 40 degrees, the wind blowing inside the narrow glass tube of a Celsius thermometer, I encountered 15 robins sitting higgledy-piggledy on concrete steps. Pecking at blue salt-streaked berries that had fallen from the juniper spreading above them. Orange breast feathers fluffed large against the cold, & all so close I could have picked each one up & held it & addressed a few warm words & put it down again. I read on the Internet (which you never experienced) that since you died in 1965, the number of overwintering robins here has increased from 1000 to 40,000. They take a chance that the winter will be mild. When you were writing, Jack, Rachel was writing about the silent spring, & these robins were very silent indeed, but Jack, it's a cold February day—when my subway train crossed the Viaduct Bridge, the Don was frozen—& all the Valentine's poems are written.

Sincerely,
Maureen

February 22

Dear Jack,

Don't you think we are most interested in dignity when we are
robbed of it, when we are in most danger of losing it? We don't want
to say we are far more interested in *indignity*, but fear takes us there.
The dignity-cloak slips off to reveal our foolish naked selves, our
inner unworthiness. But dignity can be inherited, like sterling silver,
or borrowed like golf clubs from the person beside us. Our situation
can be heightened into glory by proximity to another. *Deign & dainty*,
my dictionary tells me, are members of its word family. Ah, but
when you died, Jack, things were not dainty or dignified.

It's the same with birth—often so very difficult & messy. But don't
you think birth is part of the rosary of mysteries, its 5 strings of
10 prayers each, permission for the mind to clamshell shut on the
incomprehensible, to stop tormenting the impossible into being?
Jack, on rosary nights, always on Sundays, our family knelt on the
living-room rug & wheeled through the mysteries, Joyful, Glorious
& Sorrowful. Now the Vatican has announced a new decade of
mysteries, the *Luminous* ones, so we won't be depressed by all the sad
or unfathomable ones.

But, Jack, I don't think we can be dignified on our knees.

Sincerely,
Maureen

what she hears

                     clinks   pen scratches
chimes   underchat   her Chinese name
called across a courtyard three decades ago
someone's harmonic   she means *harmonica*
railcars thundering   at the foot of her street

                    today at lunch
her doctor friends compared
smart phone apps   she gazed
steadily into the round dot on a screen
it examined her optic nerve
another dot counted her heartbeats
a third dialed up a dead brother   no
answer   their phones not as smart as
her doctor in China   who held
her wrist for many minutes   listened
for the strength & speed of her pulses
named them   *knotted* or *choppy* or *hesitant*

                    no answer
she considers the productive & unproductive
uses of silence   in silence she questions
her inner pulses   how strongly
do they really beat   she considers
the chill silence   after a flood
after a fire   treeless cindered quiet
no response   to her questions shouted

into a prehistoric cave   so many
human   animal   avian   exoskeletal
shells & bones   lie soundless

Lull

In the several months before
marriage documents are signed
consider this newer stage of later life.
A long lucky lull, ten to fifteen years

between parent loss and sibling
departures, into which love pours.
How high is the degree of gratitude
and how deep into the heart's core

has good fortune settled?
The displaced beauty of that outdoor
art installation—rebar sliding off
Muskoka granite into tall
grass. Rust within a forest: which
will endure? How our spirits

habituate to dread—
fears aborning, marrying,
widowing. Seal official papers with
resin, tie them with grosgrain,
set them inside an old

blue-flowered tea tin.
Take the tin to the aspen
in the field made fertile
with guano and leaf,
nestle it into the tree's
anchoring roots.

Are you ladies lost? 1

asks one of the men as we stand staring up
into the bare-branched tree at the end of our street.
No, we say, *no: we're looking at the robin.*

Robin singing plumply from a February branch:
dawn song, a run of high notes that trill
upwards, back to the lost sounds—sounds of the bone

or bamboo flute, of a sharp shovel cutting into turf,
whir of the spinning wheel, electric typewriter.
Why have you come back so soon, we ask the robin,

or did you never leave? The two guys look at us
with concern. One says, *The men won gold
this morning.* "Our team" on a distant frozen rink.

We slip and crackle our way across ice patches,
up and down decaying snowbanks. The two men
themselves seem a bit lost, but we are grateful

for the return of birdsong and their kindness.
We go back home for showers and laundry and washing
the week's radishes and carrots and pears.

Sunday morning, last day of the Olympics,
but we are more warmed by the roundness
and cheer-up song from the tree

beside the train tracks, by the gush of hot water
and the love cries that spilled into our night's sleep.
What am I here for? asks my friend's elderly mother,

impatient to die. *Just to notice one beautiful thing a day,*
she tells her. A few blocks over, the carillon at the Russian
Orthodox church rings. A ripple of white

swirls in transparent ice over a driveway puddle.
Two bouquets of orange-streaked
yellow tulips, winter sunset in a vase.

Are you ladies lost? 2

oh no we are not lost   we are just hesitating   under the leafless
trees   wishing we were in New York or Málaga or
Melbourne   we are finding it hard to move as we are wishing
Franco had come to a more deserving end   not to mention
Henry Kissinger or the Bushes Senior & Junior   & that other
newer one   we are assembling our spray cans to spray graffiti
on railway sidings   to repel DOT-111 railcars   oh no we are
not lost   but we do have a kind of science-fiction look on our
faces   not lost   but perhaps losing   well, maybe a little
lost   but pausing to count the moths & ladybugs   one
of whom I found in my hydroponic lettuce this week   you are a
local ladybug I said to the colourful pill-like corpse   you were born
& died here   which makes you friendly & heroic   & well-fed
we are scanning the sky for drones   as everyone must these
days   the animal extinction count is troubling us   oh no
we are not very lost   but we are grateful for your concern

Late Love Song, with an Orange: A Cento

We who are paired—
scarcely talking, thoughts pass between us.
We had to drink spilled moon from the lake for courage.
Nothing was speaking to me, but I offered and all was well.
I married her with my face upright to the sky.

My glass I lift at six o'clock, my darling,
my heart of mayonnaise.
We are in easy understanding.
This summerbed is soft with ring upon ring
upon ring of wedding, the kind
that doesn't clink upon contact.
You can tell
I hear it, too, by the look on my face:
that inaudible thumping.
Now I'm a bird in the nest of your lap.
When you show yourself to the woman
you love, you don't know your fear—
happiness is a kind of fear.

here, now here, closer like a mouth
opening and closing, opening and closing—
naked
as a heap of clothes, still whispering *undress me,*
body hair glistening with a thousand arts,
I offer a necklace of tears, orgasms, words
or the soft babble of a kiss.

O for a life of Kisses
Instead of painting volcanoes!
joy in my mouth like a peppered bird.
This means laughter
or wings.
I will be standing at the edge
of that fathomless crowd with an orange for you—
full, the way a woman stands
when you meet her at an unexpected corner.

aubade

softer than amethyst   but crystalline & unfamiliar
is waking in the creak   of this borrowed bed with you
the coldest night this winter   has scratched

a ferny pointillism on every window   I rise
to photograph frosted glass against the neighbour's
red brick wall   against the glacier-blue sky

against the street's rooflines   return to your side
show you   cupid's icy arrows   you put
your thumb to my forehead   release

the night visitors   we have both dreamed of our sisters
dawn vanishes slowly   on a February morning
the lovers' reluctance   to rip open the day's envelope

& accept   its aching temperatures   but
we are lucky   our day holds   no whips or war wounds
surgeries or life sentences   displacement settles

we recall who we are   what we must accomplish
this day   O valentine   a name with a farewell in it
a salute to worthiness & departure   juncos appear

in dozens at the feeder   ice swells inside the sliding door
I broke my promise   didn't overlook the conventions
of doily hearts & chocolate truffles   my misdeed born of love

where does my love stop?

daily my love stops
traces the sorrow segments
etched into the turtle's shell

stops to count how many sunflower
petals on a tall stalk   the sudden
way breath can cease   then starts

filling the wild gourd with clean water as
Cyclone Pam, Category 5, keeps
pouring & pouring & pouring

hospital operating rooms filling
halfway up their walls with muddy
water   stops as you did

this morning   in the kitchen
the pinecone opened & small
angry seeds fell out

scattered   all over the floor & somehow
sprouted tenderness in the cracks
between ceramic tiles   love starts

breathing again because of the wet
lilac branches   starts despite the dynamite
stick of injustice   the bridge

to compassion intact   we can still cross
my love re-clad   in a length of deep blue
cotton   hemmed with silver thread

NOTES

Inside My Quietness After Frank O'Hara's "In Memory of My Feelings" in *The Collected Poems of Frank O'Hara,* edited by Donald Allen (University of California Press, 1995), and Margaret Christakos's "Lake" in *Her Paraphernalia: On Motherlines, Sex, Blood, Loss & Selfies* (Book*hug, 2016).

The Horses, the Sorrow, the Umbilicus "The horses were turned loose in the child's sorrow" is the first line of Carolyn Forché's *Blue Hour* (HarperCollins, 2003); "Looking to the left, looking to the right. She—" is the last line of Gail Scott's *Heroine* (Coach House, 1987).

April 1 lune Though similar to the three-line 5/7/5 syllable pattern of a haiku, the lune's is 5/3/5.

How Spring Begins "Tags of songs, like salvaged buttons" and "Is it for miracles / We live?" are from James Schuyler's *Collected Poems* (Farrar, Straus and Giroux, 1993).

Ancestors After "Good Dog, Bad Dog I, II and III," from Anne Carson's *Float* (McClelland & Stewart, 2016); "each and every moment's a shortcut" is from Bei Dao's "New Year," from *Landscape over Zero,* translated by David Hinton with Yanbing Chen (New Directions, 1996).

Twenty Naked Selves Also after Frank O'Hara's "In Memory of My Feelings."

Sotto Voce Written in response to the International Contemporary Ensemble production of *the whisper opera* by David Lang, Soundstreams, Toronto, February/March, 2015; "After the breath stops the words listen" is from "A Fake Novel about the Life of Arthur Rimbaud: Plato's Marmalade," and "All the way down past the future. The words go swimming past you as if they were blue fish . . ." is from "A Textbook of Poetry, 21," both in Jack Spicer's *my vocabulary did this to me: The Collected Poetry of Jack Spicer* (Wesleyan, 2008).

In Solitary As his final wish, Rubin "Hurricane" Carter published a plea in the *New York Daily News* that convict David McCallum's case be reopened, and that he be freed. McCallum was freed on October 15, 2014 after serving almost thirty years for a murder he did not commit. The phrase "innocent as witches" is from James Schuyler's "Seeking," again, in his *Collected Poems.*

Keep it Dark The poem's title and the name "the Queer Quartette" were copied from anonymous handwritten text under snapshots in the *Fan the Flames* photography exhibit curated by Sophie Hackett at the Art Gallery of Ontario (June 18 to September 7, 2014) as part of World Pride celebrations; US poet Joanne Kyger to interviewer Paul Watsky: "Robert Duncan and the San Francisco poets used Greek mythology a lot. They talked about the gods and goddesses as if they were sitting there on the windowsill all the time . . ." (*Jung Journal: Culture & Psyche* 7:3, Summer 2013).

A State of Undress The poem's italicized words are not all exact quotations; some are approximations of comments made during the artists' lifetimes, copied from the exhibition material for *1920s Modernism in Montreal: The Beaver Hall Group* at the Art Gallery of Hamilton, February 20 to May 8, 2016.

Fearless This poem is a collage of lines from participants' work in the University of Toronto's SCS 1705 course during the Spring 2016 semester: Deborah Barndt, Jennifer Burns, Sue Folinsbee, Marlene Kadar, May Ann Kainola, Adam Kidd, Maya Stewart Pathak, and Don Smith. It's dedicated to them, and their fear-conquering spirits, with so many thanks.

High Water Mark The quotation is drawn from a conversation I had with Anishinaabe artist Bonnie Devine during the exhibit *Before and After the*

Horizon: Anishinaabe Artists of the Great Lakes, at the Art Gallery of Ontario, Toronto, 2014. Many thanks to her for allowing me to quote her here.

The climate is pretty. I wrote everything on it. The poem's title borrows the first two lines from John Ashbery's "As Someone Who Likes Travel" (*The New Yorker,* May 23, 2016).

Derailment Ode Several Cars Long The "Abundance GTA" ceremony was conducted by the group The Soul of the Mother, with members Cyndi White, Jackie Ryan, and Vivi Silverstein on October 15, 2016.

Sonnenizio on the Unseen The sonnenizio is a blended sonnet form invented by US poet Kim Addonizio. She requires the poem to start with a line borrowed from another poet. One word from that first line is then used in each of the succeeding 13 lines. The sonnenizio must end with a rhymed couplet. I've taken liberties with the word "see" and use variations of it or use words that contain it as a syllable. My first line is taken from Bernadette Mayer's "Incandescent War Poem Sonnet" in the 25th Anniversary Edition of *Sonnets* (Tender Buttons, 2014).

Preventorium Toronto's High Park Forest School was started in 1915 and was closed in the early 1960s. The text under a photograph of schoolchildren at outdoor desks reads: "health … and knowledge … both are the lot of the scores of happy children who are privileged to attend the Forest School in High Park. Here the repairing of wasted little bodies is a matter of prime concern to the staff…" (*The Globe,* Toronto, July 7, 1922; photo by James & Son, Photographers, 440 Manning Avenue, Toronto).

motherspeak "Take not / away from me the small fires / I burn in the memory of love" is from John Wieners' "A poem for cock suckers" in *Supplication: Selected Poems of John Wieners* (Wave Books, 2015).

newborn "Dreams reveal / how much in danger we are" is from John Wieners' "July 25," again, in *Supplication*.

Apollo After Joanne Kyger's question, "Do they have classes / on how to die?" in "Throw Away Mind" from *About Now: Collected Poems* (National Poetry Foundation, 2007).

dolorosa MOAB (the "Massive Ordnance Air Blast" but also called the "mother of all bombs"), dropped by US forces on Afghanistan in April 2017, was supposed to be the second-deadliest weapon, next to the nuclear bomb (*The Guardian*, April 15, 2017).

Not Enough The title is indebted to Amiri Baraka's "Wise 2" from *S O S: Poems 1961–2013* (Grove, 2014).

Dear Jack These letters are addressed to Jack Spicer.

Late Love Song, with an Orange: A Cento The cento is a poetic form entirely made up of lines from poems by other poets; its name comes from the Latin word for "patchwork." Sources, sometimes in very slightly altered form, are cited in line order: Jane Munro, Sue Goyette, Joanne Kyger, Muriel Rukeyser, Erín Moure, John Berryman, Mary Ruefle, Joanne Kyger, Brenda Shaughnessy, Hillary Gravendyk, Laura Kasischke, Catherine Graham, Maleea Acker, Catherine Graham, Barry Dempster, Nicole Brossard, Alicia Suskin Ostriker, Barry Dempster, Mary Ruefle, Maleea Acker, Erín Moure, Mary Ruefle, and Dionne Brand.

where does my love stop? "This is where my love, somehow, stops" is from Jack Spicer's "Six Poems for *Poetry* Chicago" in *my vocabulary did this to me: The Collected Poetry of Jack Spicer* (Wesleyan, 2008).

ACKNOWLEDGEMENTS

My thanks to the editors of these journals for selecting earlier versions of these poems for publication:

"Into the Humber River," "The Missing Island," and "Keep It Dark" in *Contemporary Verse 2*;

"motherspeak," "Twenty Naked Selves" in *La Presa*;

"Sonnenizio on the Unseen" in *Literary Review of Canada*;

"Staying Away from the Grand River" in *Plenitude*;

"693 Cemetery Road" in *Poetry Pause,* the League of Canadian Poets' daily poetry dispatch;

"Sotto Voce" and "aubade" in *Southword* (Ireland);

"bolt of fabric" in *The Fiddlehead*;

"The Horses, the Sorrow, the Umbilicus" in *The Malahat Review*;

"693 Cemetery Road" in *The Puritan*;

"A Taxonomy of Trouble," "Phonograph," and "In Solitary" in *The Windsor Review*;

and *"Are you ladies lost? 1"* and *"Are you ladies lost? 2"* in *White Wall Review.*

Thanks to the editors of these anthologies for including these poems:

"Derailment Ode Several Cars Long," "speaking for sky," and "Our Own Myths" in *Abundance: A Harvest of Texts for the Pickering Lands* (Gesture Press and Fieldnotes, 2016);

"Preventorium" in *High Art: Poetry Walk in High Park* (Gesture Press, 2016);

"The Missing Island" in *Reading the Don* (Gesture Press, 2015);

"Late Love Song, with an Orange: A Cento" in *In Fine Form,* 2nd Edition, edited by Kate Braid and Sandy Shreve (Caitlin, 2016), and in *Love Me True,* edited by Fiona Tinwei Lam and Jane Silcott (Caitlin, 2018).

Gratitude to:

Ruth Kazdan, for inspiration, support, constancy, daily delight;

John Barton, for supremely skillful editing attention to every word and this book as a whole;

Ronna Bloom, whose work, laughter, and attentive listening gladden me;

Sandra Campbell, for organizing the arts-filled and heart-filling "Abundance GTA" event in fall, 2017 to honour the Pickering Lands and for inviting me to contribute poems, some of which appear here;

Steven Carter, for generosity, for inspiration, insight into so many poets' work, and a special friendship;

Sue Chenette, for friendship and for thoughtful in-depth poetic discussions;

Barry Dempster, wise friend, generous editor, and long-time mentor;

Beth Follett, for her vision, her generosity, and her support;

Amy Gottlieb, for a beautiful line in *"Are You Ladies Lost? 1"*;

Sonja Greckol, Al-Andaluz friend, for a crackerjack reading of this book;

Joan Guenther, meticulous and inspired photographer-poet;

Helen Guri, for her editorial discernment, challenges, and encouragement;

Fiona Tinwei Lam, for *croquembouche*, for long companionship and encouragement on the poetry road;

Hoa Nguyen, for her warmth and poetics, and for creating the inspiring community where so many of these poems emerged;

Alayna Munce, editor, advisor, friend;

Joanne Page, with aching delight in the memory of her generosity, warmth, and brilliance;

Arleen Paré, wonderful new poetry colleague and friend;

Ruth Roach Pierson, for close reading of this manuscript and years of companionship in poetry, film, and travel;

Vivek Shraya, exemplar of support, creativity, courage, dedication;

Jane Springer, long-time friend, first and continuing editor, whose talks about writing, politics, and love inspire and sustain me.

Special thanks to all my walking, writing, and floating groups, to each member singly and the groups collectively, for their care for the written word, wisdom, and friendship:

huge thanks, all the way back, and still, to The Miss Vickies (Linda Briskin, Jennifer Rudder, Liz Ukrainetz, Barb Young);

The Thursday Night Group (Barry Dempster, Maureen Scott Harris, Liz Ukrainetz, Jim Nason);

The Victoria University Group (Alan Ackerman, Allan Briesmaster, Andrew Brooks, Sue Chenette, Carla Hartsfield, Carleton Wilson, Dorothy Sandler-Glick, Jeremy Harman, Leif Vaage, Pierre L'Abbé, Richard Green, Robert Johnson, Ruth Roach Pierson, and with very special thanks to John Reibetanz);

The Grenadier Group (Ann Irwin, Pramila Aggarwal, Jean Unda, and honourary member, Tracy Westell);

The Electronic Garret (the virtual group of electric feminist poets started by the dauntless Tanis MacDonald);

The Floating Readers (Sue Chenette, Steven Carter, Jaclyn Piudik);

The Lost River Poets (Maureen Scott Harris, Nicholas Power, Julie Roorda, Sue Chenette, Dilys Leman, Anita Lahey), who have made our river walking tours so much fun, with special thanks to Helen Mills of Lost Rivers Toronto who suggested the idea of river poetry walks and is responsible for the presence of creeks and streams and rivers in this book);

The Honeymoon Bay participants (Kate Braid, Lorna Crozier, Sandra Campbell, Fiona Lam, Judy Leblanc, JoAnn McCaig, Jane Munro, Susan Olding, Arleen Paré, Elizabeth Philips);

and The Ireland Park Poets (Nicholas Power and Catherine Graham).

Dedications:

"With a fingernail" is for Steven Carter;

"ajoupa 1" is for Monica Voss;

"Dearest friend," and "The Ballad for a Good Night's Sleep" are in memory of Joanne Page;

"octopus" is for Barb Young;

"speaking for sky," "Derailment Ode Several Cars Long," "Our Own Myths," and "Little Rouge Creek" are all for the people of the expropriated Pickering lands, Ontario.

Maureen Hynes's poetry collection *Rough Skin* (Wolsak and Wynn, 1995), won the League of Canadian Poets' Gerald Lampert Award for best first book of poetry by a Canadian. Her most recent collection, *The Poison Colour* (Pedlar Press, 2015), was shortlisted in 2016 for both the Pat Lowther and Raymond Souster Awards. Her poetry has been included in over twenty-five anthologies, including twice in *The Best Canadian Poetry in English,* and in *The Best of the Best Canadian Poetry in English* (Tightrope Books, 2017). Maureen is poetry editor for *Our Times* magazine. She lives in Toronto.